AF380016

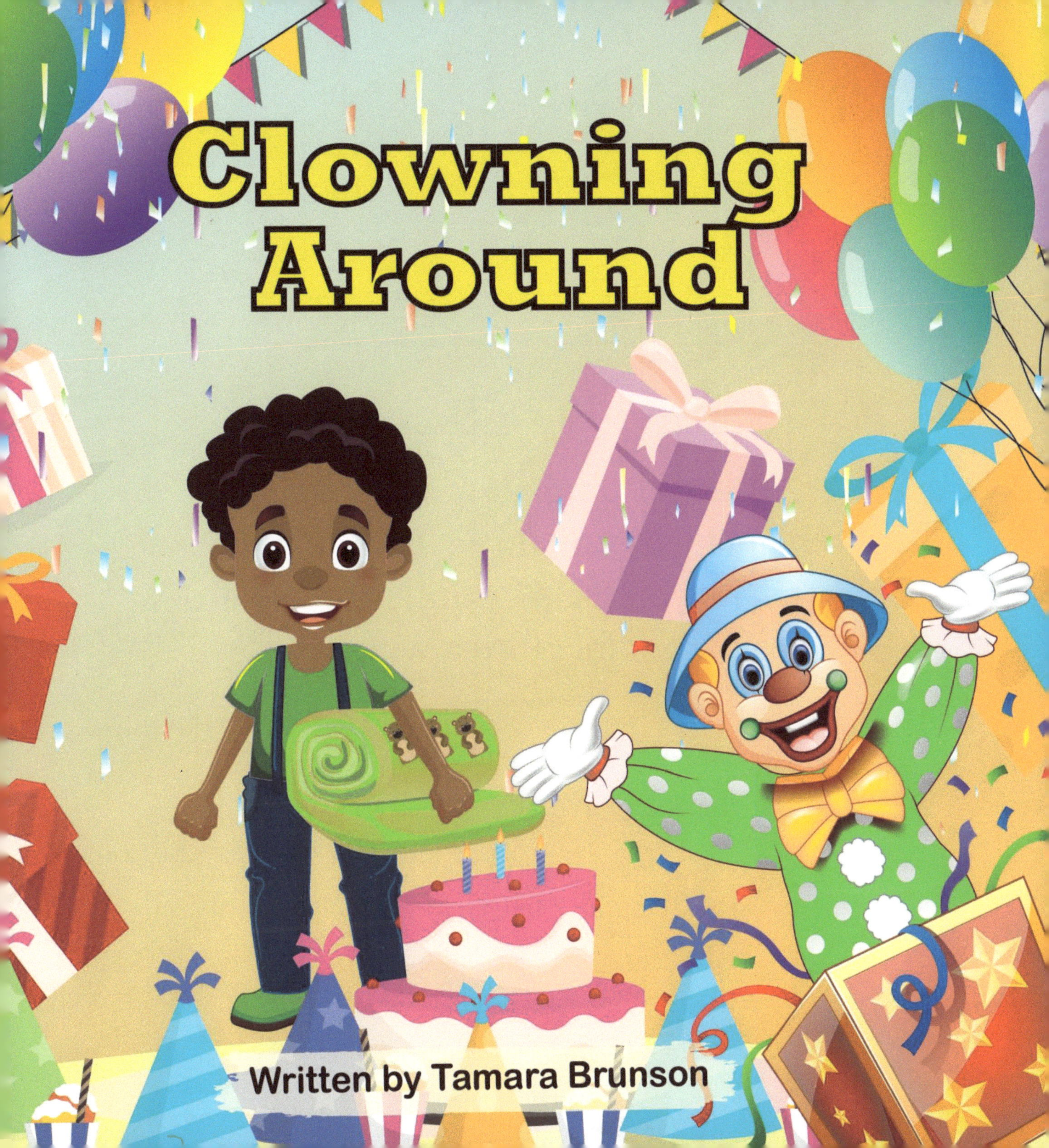

Clowning
Around

Written by Tamara Brunson

My Dedication

I dedicate this story to my kids,
Tierra, Vaughn, and Terrence.
Mommy loves you three with all my heart.
Thank you for allowing me to share
our special stories with others.

Love you forever and ever,

Mommy

Hi! My name is Ryan.
My birthday is in two days, and my
mom is getting a clown for my party.
But clowns scare me.

She says clowns are fun and silly.
But all I see is a man
who has paint on his face,
big shoes on his feet,
big clothes on his body,
nd a funny-sounding voice when he talks.

Well, today is my birthday party,
and the clown is on his way.

All I can think about is
how I can kick and run
when he comes close to me.

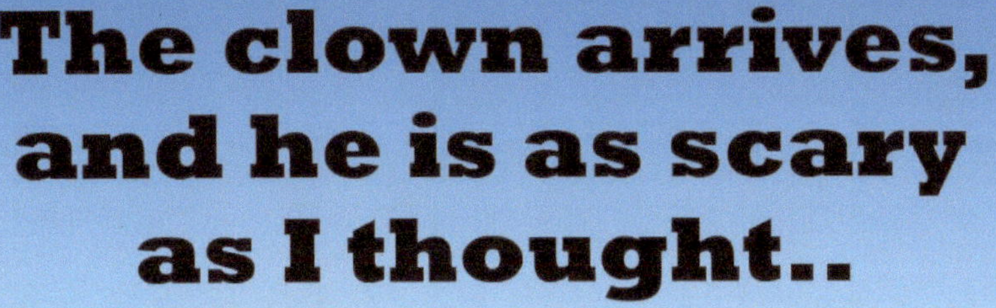

The clown arrives,
and he is as scary
as I thought..

But I am having fun!
This birthday is the best birthday
I've ever had —
in the four years of my life,
that is.

HAPPY
BIRTHDAY

And guess what?
The clown turns out to be
my daddy!
How cool is that?

ow it's time to start planning
or next year's birthday party.

APPY
RTHDAY

Let's see what my daddy
will be next year.
k, my friends. Until next time,
catch you later!

The End

About the Author

Tamara Brunson is a mother of three
who lives in Rockland County, New York.
Her passion for writing started with her firstborn son,
and continued with her youngest son,
as their past experiences as toddlers
and elementary-grade students
helped shape the focus of her writing.
She loves to write children's stories and
enjoys reading them to her sons to make them laugh.
Their enthusiasm has encouraged her to publish her stories
and share them with other children around the world.
She hopes families will enjoy them
and plans to publish more books in the future.

CPSIA information can be obtained
at www.ICGtesting.com
Printed in the USA
LVHW070154210721
693275LV00003B/55